UNBECOMING

Tiana Harewood

Copyright © 2021 Tiana Harewood

All rights reserved.

ISBN: 978-1-7320181-3-6

All rights reserved. No part of this publication may be reproduced, stored, or transmitted in any form or by any means – whether electronic, mechanical, photocopy, auditory, graphic, without written permission from both the publisher and author, except in the case of brief excerpts used in critical articles and reviews.
Email:broadhervillage@gmail.com

Legal Disclaimer: Tiana Harewood takes no responsibility for the decisions made by readers after reading this book.
This book is for inspirational and motivational purposes only.

Scripture marked NIV are taken from THE HOLY BIBLE, NEW INTERNATIONAL VERSION®, NIV® Copyright © 1973, 1978, 1984, 2011 by Biblica, Inc.® Used by permission. All rights reserved worldwide.

Scripture marked NKJV taken from the New King James Version®. Copyright © 1982 by Thomas Nelson. Used by permission. All rights reserved.

Scripture quotations marked NLT are taken from the *Holy Bible*, New Living Translation, copyright © 1996, 2004, 2015 by Tyndale House Foundation. Used by permission of Tyndale House Publishers, Inc., Carol Stream, Illinois 60188. All rights reserved.

Cover Design by Chassittie Adams
chassitieg@gmail.com
Interior Illustrations by Kienda Koonce
Livefree070@gmail.com

Cover Photo by Studio EnVogue Photography
www.studioenvogue.com studioenvogue@gmail.com

Published by A.T. Destiny Awaits Group LLC
atdestinyawaitsgroup@gmail.com

MY DEDICATION

As damaged as I am, this is the purest version of myself I've ever seen. So it makes me question my definition of damaged or perhaps the definition that I've been taught. Unbecoming is about redefining your life for what it really is. Not what society says and not what tradition says. It's about peeling back all of the layers that we've put on throughout the years of life experiences and challenges, internal and external. It's about unbecoming everything we thought was good, to be who we were always meant to be.

This book is dedicated to those in transition. The people who are exhausted from wearing other people's garments. The people who are not sure of where to start undressing. The damaged, yet pure. The broken, yet whole. The naked, yet free. This is for you. Unbecome.

TABLE OF CONTENTS

Chapter One
        Yesterday
              2

Chapter Two
        Novice
              8

Chapter Three
        Detox
              16

Chapter Four
        Mirrors
              26

Chapter Five
        Giants
              32

Chapter Six
        Passions
              42

Chapter Seven
        Today
              49

Chapter Eight
        Diary
              55

PREFACE

Many of us are so focused on becoming the person God has called us to be, but I genuinely believe that we don't need to become someone else for God to be pleased with us. He's given us everything that we need to please Him. We only need to tap into the person hidden behind all of the layers of stuff we've obtained throughout life.

"For we are His workmanship, created in Christ Jesus for good works, which God prepared beforehand that we should walk in them." Ephesians 2:10.

YESTERDAY

"Yesterday unraveled is the compilation of complications that contribute to mysteries of your history."

YESTERDAY

"Yesterday unraveled is the compilation of complications that contribute to the mysteries of your history."

So yesterday, I cried. I sat in my bathroom with the door closed and the light off, and I cried. I was angry because I was not where I wanted to be in life. I had a good job. My kids were amazing. I was busy taking care of a household. I was in school. Everything, externally, was fine. At least, that is what could have been perceived by anyone taking a look at my situation. I thought I was being productive by being busy, but I was just being efficient. The truth was that if I had sat down somewhere, I probably would have been more productive because I wasn't present. I had learned to function at a very minimal capacity completing the basics of life to get to the next day. There was more in me; that I knew for sure.

Lesson: Being busy isn't always a sign of productivity. It's a must to understand the definitions of effective and efficient and to decipher between the two.

I woke up yesterday morning, did my usual morning things, made lunches for the girls, dressed us, brushed our teeth, and fixed our hair. I took the girls to their respective places and headed to work. Work was work. I got off, picked up the girls, made dinner, gave baths, said prayers, and put them to bed. The day was totally normal, but I was less than pleased.

I felt incomplete. I felt like there was more to Tiana than just being a good mom and student and girlfriend, and I was not living up to my potential. I was settling because to everybody else, I was doing good for myself. I invested in everyone else's perception of me and my situation, although I wasn't being the person I needed to be.

    I was impatient in every aspect of my life. What people didn't see was me getting frustrated and yelling at the kids for doing simple things like spilling a drink on the floor. They didn't hear the judgmental thoughts I'd think about people who would offend me. They didn't see the angry girl throwing her laptop at the floor because her classes were getting the best of her. I was not the Tiana that I knew or the Tiana I wanted to be. I had become this ball of frustration, anger, and anxiety.

    At this point in my life, I was effective. I was getting things done. I was moving through life, but life wasn't moving through me. I exerted so much energy to every other place in my life that I would forget to stand in the mirror. I didn't know who I was to me; I just knew who I was to other people. I looked at every person and situation around me and how they affected me versus looking inward and trying to see how I affected them.

    I remember getting so frustrated at work because my manager was not doing her job like I felt that she should've been doing her job. She was lazy and always put her work on other people. Then she'd take the credit when upper management was around. That really ground my gears. For me, it was the principle of the matter. Well, that's what I told myself. When you're given a position of power, you should lead by example. Simple. The problem was that through my arrogance, I had not taken the time to learn from her. It was my desire to be right and in control which created a barrier that prevented me from becoming a better me. I put so much energy into critiquing her that I didn't see that she was in the position that I wanted to be in someday. Therefore, I needed to get inside of myself because even though I disagreed with her execution, she had something that I didn't. I had tricked myself into thinking that she was a problem when I put that title on her. She was simply being her. I had no right to label her a problem, therefore creating this animosity towards her, which ultimately only affected ME!

So much energy was wasted during my encounter with that manager, when all along I was the problem. Needless to say, I failed that test. Furthermore, it's a true testament of how wasteful we can be when we're just being effective, just getting things done to mark them off our checklists versus taking the time to ask God how to be as effective as we can with what and who He has given us.

It's overwhelming to think back to how I conducted myself just because of ignorance. I didn't know that there was a reason behind the fire that burned inside of me when I saw her doing something that even I had done, just in a different context. Maybe I didn't take credit for other people's work, but I was definitely not as authentic as I thought I was.

Not only did I turn outward for the reasons behind my actions, but I also neglected the innermost issues I had within myself. I hated the fact that I couldn't speak up when it was necessary. I hated that I would internalize things that I was supposed to confront and work out. I thought that I was doing other people a favor by holding things in, but secretly I was burning on the inside. The internal flames produced a smoke cloud over my worldview and made me think that avoiding my deepest, most evident concerns was the way to keep the peace. At that time, I didn't realize how toxic that thought pattern was to my growth. I believed that if I said how I truly felt, I would've been met with all of the reasons why my feelings weren't valid.

Truth be told, the fear that I felt was probably valid based on my past experiences. There was a possibility that I would've been met with everything I expected, but I should've never allowed that to dictate my truth.

Lesson: There will be times when we are not accepted with open arms. Our feelings won't be validated every time we share them, but don't let that stop you from sharing, in turn, causing your smoke cloud to form and alter your viewpoint of God, yourself, and others.

So, yesterday I cried. I couldn't look at myself in the mirror. I refused to look at the horrible person that I had become. I allowed my emotions to be embedded into my character. I was the anger that I exerted. I was the impatience that I displayed. I was the pride that I harbored. I was not always like this, though, which frustrated me even more. I was the type of person that genuinely loved no matter the circumstances. If someone wronged me, I'd take the time to empathize, understanding that it's much bigger than me. I'd question what THEY were going through instead of taking things personally. In my opinion, at the time, that's how people should be, but I let anger set in, and it consumed my spirit. Yesterday, I took on Anger, Impatience, and Arrogance. That's not the most attractive thing to confess, but it's real, and it was yesterday.

At this point, I realized that I was heavy. I carried so much weight from my past. I had packed a bag of my stuff, along with other people's stuff, and chose to move through life carrying it because I thought this is what you're supposed to do when you're evolving or developing into who you were meant to be. No one told me that I have a choice during this life of whether to take or leave something. I thought that if it was offered that I should just take it because if something was presented to me, it meant that I was chosen for that task, right? Wrong. So wrong.

Here's the thing, we always have a choice. God even gave us a choice of whether to accept His gift of salvation. Now, if our Creator gives us choices, what makes us think that we have to accept everything that presents itself to us. Every experience that I went through presented new ideas of who I thought I should be, qualities I felt I should have to be successful. Little did I know, I was just making my cross heavier to bear.

We already have things that are attached to us when we are birthed into this realm. Yes, there are things that are automatically assigned to you, so you will have to go through some things. Yes, some things will shape you without forewarning; however, we have to understand that we don't have to cling to everyone's perception of us. We don't have to take on labels to make us feel like we fit somewhere. Sometimes the shoes do not fit, and that's okay.

I remember being in a group with some ladies, and we were sharing our troubles. The ladies exposed themselves, and I exposed parts of me that weren't really me. I said that I dealt with pride because I didn't want to be wrong. In actuality, it wasn't so much of pride FOR ME; it was more so; I was a serial perfectionist, not because I wanted someone to say that I was right and give me praises, but so that I can continue flying under the radar. I misdiagnosed myself because I had carried so much weight for so long. At that moment, I wanted to relate, so I reached into the bag I carried and pulled out the wrong thing.

This situation happens more often than we think. It is easier to identify with other people's hurt, so we use that as a point of contact, thinking we're being effective when we're just being efficient. We're identifying issues, but are they really our issues? Or are they the issues that are just sitting on the top of the bag? Is there a connection of purpose, or is it only a connection of pain?

NOVICE

"To begin is to bypass all things that say it's too hard, it's too much, or you're not enough. It's to be launched into oblivion allowing God to guide you."

Guilt and shame were the main events of my life's party. I was supposed to know better. Aren't I smart enough not to put myself in a situation that would cause me to hurt? What happened to me? How did I get here? I'm sure you may have asked yourself these questions or similar questions. Let me tell you about a girl I knew who put on more weight than she could handle.

It didn't happen overnight. The seed was planted when she was very young (I would put an age on it, but it's not important). She was deemed to be so tiny, pretty, and smart by others. She loved to dance and liked to be the center of attention. Oh, how bright did her light shine throughout her childhood. Did I mention how sassy she was as well? She was very much a born leader. However, her heart was so big and sensitive. She'd cry if she disappointed someone. She never dismissed people's feelings. She was very much aware, despite her age. Her mother struggled as a single parent, but she never knew it. Despite her awareness, she never felt like anything was missing. She felt loved. They lived with friends and family for awhile, bouncing around countless times. They traveled a whole lot, and she grew to like the adventure. It wasn't until she started school that things began to shift. She was still tiny, pretty, and smart, but now she was exposed to these other perceptions. These other ideas of who she was or who she was to become.

She was fortunate enough to get to the second grade without experiencing how other people's perceptions can indeed affect a person. I don't believe that she knew what the term "bully" meant at the time, but it was what she experienced. She had just started a new school, and she was ready to shine her light brightly as she had always done. Her mom and aunt walked her to her classroom, hugged her goodbye, and off she went on another adventure. Of course, she was nervous, but she was definitely a "big girl" now. She had this! She walked in, and everything was to her liking. She loved her teacher and made a couple of friends within her classroom, but it wasn't until she met Jealousy, Envy, and Hate that she realized that she'd graduated to a new level of big girldom. Jealousy, Envy, and Hate were the popular girls in their grade. They did everything together, and everyone wanted to be connected to them, including the little girl.

One day the little girl and her friend named *Rejection* were at recess, and the little girl decided that this was the day she'd make three new friends. She approached the girls and was greeted with more than enough attitude to make her feel as if something was wrong with her. She asked *Rejection* what was wrong with her and the reply was, "you're just not like them." The little girl thought to herself, "well, what do I have to do to be like them?" Now, I could continue with her story, but how it ends doesn't matter because this is the moment when who she was, her original state, was not enough for her. She didn't understand that her value did not lie in the hands of *Rejection* or the other three naysayers that she'd soon encounter again later in life. *Rejection* was correct, she wasn't like them, but somehow she took that response as a challenge to become everything that she was not. All it took was a single statement to make her feel like she was missing out on something.

The little girl had not yet tapped into even the smallest portion of potential that she held within her soul because it is our nature to seek outward no matter the cost. We seek, we find, and we keep whatever pleases our immediate need, and we never take the time to take an inventory of what we have before looking for other things. Therefore, we become weighed down with ideas and motives that were never supposed to be embedded in us. So, when it's time for us to move forward into our purpose, we don't know which way to go or which idea to pursue.

Lesson: Our generation is often so focused on all things new that we discard the old things as if they're ineffective or somehow they've lost their value. We want to be innovators in every aspect of life. We don't mind faking it until we make it because we're fascinated with how things make us look to the public. What if I told you that you already possess all that you need to be successful? Instead of groveling, at the first sight or word of something new. Take inventory of your old things and experiment with ways to utilize ideas you've already produced before moving on to something new. I'm sure you're going to find it challenging but do it anyway. It's easy to look outward and identify things we don't have instead of looking inward and identifying easy things to produce with what we already have.

I am not excluded. Before now, I spent a large portion of my time looking outward for inward validation. I excelled in school. I excelled at work. I didn't mess up. I was calculated with a lot of my decisions. If I failed, it's because I wanted to fail. If I excelled, it's because I wanted to excel. You didn't tell me what I could or could not do because whatever I wanted, I got. This personal concept served as a barrier between who I was and who I wanted to be. I wanted to be right by any means necessary. I wanted to have the right principles, the right persona, the right mindset, the right verbiage, the right everything. The sad thing is that I was very wrong a lot of times. I had formed an idea of what all these rights were by looking at others, their persona, exploring their thought patterns, examining their verbiage, and not once did I ask God to reveal to me what was already right about me. I remember crying while I was driving specifically, asking God to change my identity because this unbecoming revelation came to me a lot earlier than when I first started writing this book. It came when I realized that all of my efforts to be right had backfired and left me alone with all my faux rightness.

Now, we've met Jealousy, Envy, Hate, and Rejection. The little girl struggled through that school year. She became closer and closer with *Rejection* every day, though. They shared many commonalities. They identified with each other when she'd walk into a room and hear whispers; she knew that something negative was being said about her. They identified with each other when she had her first crush, but all she could think about were the mean things Jealousy, Envy, and Hate planted inside of her head. They identified with each other when she made friends and was introduced to Betrayal.

Betrayal made a storming entrance in middle school. At this time, the young lady made friends with who she trusted and they did everything together. She loved these girls, each in their own special way. She found out that one of her friends had said some mean things about her and she decided to confront her. They were sitting in the hallway, and the young lady was boiling on the inside because *Rejection* was telling her that she should've known better. She blurts out to her friend, "how can you sleep at night knowing that you just talk about people," and away they went. Weightless words were thrown around, and nothing was resolved because she was fighting with Jealousy, Envy, Hate, and not Betrayal; with *Rejection* on her side; she was bound to lose.

Lesson: Betrayal isn't meant to be a constant adversary; however, when we encounter it, we continuously fight against it with words and fists as if that's how we beat it. Betrayal is not outward; it's something that is internal. We feel betrayed because we trusted. We feel betrayed because we loved. We feel betrayed because we did what we thought was right, and it wasn't reciprocated. Who says that life is all about reciprocity? We can't expect someone to reciprocate something that they don't know. So what do we do WHEN we are betrayed? Keep loving. Keep trusting. You don't get betrayed by doing something wrong, so why would you switch up? Betrayal is a test of your goodness. Don't combat a test of goodness with bad things like paranoia, insecurity, and trust issues because then you'd take them on, just as the young lady did.

By the time the young lady made it to high school, she had Jealousy, Envy, Hate, Betrayal, Trust Issues, Paranoia, Insecurity, and her friend *Rejection*. She had gone through at least two to three more schools. She entered a new school with new faces and new perceptions. Not many people liked her because she was intentionally stand-offish. She was tired of being taken advantage of, and she wasn't going to let history repeat itself. She had found her own style, and she wore it well. There were only a handful of people that she liked and supported, and she was okay with that. She found excuses for the company that she kept. She was guarded because she had been hurt (Betrayal, Trust Issues, Paranoia). She didn't care what anybody else thought about her because they didn't matter (Rejection, Insecurity). So, she walked through high school doing all she could to be "right" to prove to Jealousy, Envy, and Hate that she could be what they said she couldn't be. She graduated in the top ten percent of her class. She was class president. She won best dressed. She participated in dual enrollment. Then, boom! She gets pregnant her senior year in high school. As right as she was, how could she be so wrong?

Like the young lady, we'd love to blame the people who left us in whatever state we find ourselves in, but it wouldn't be accurate. For the person that I thought I was, blaming others made the most sense because I was right. It was my mother's fault because she should have taught me about that part of life. It was the men in my life's fault because they were present but absent. Somebody in my family had to know that certain things would come up, and no one tried to prepare me. How awful does that sound? It was real to me, though. I took on the task of making myself who I was meant to be, which was well above my pay grade and skill level, and blaming my surroundings for not completing this God-only task.

Lesson: My friend, trust me, it's well above yours as well. Let God be all that He is to You. Allow him to be your Right. Let Him be your Creator because He is! Let Him create in you and through you.

The little girl would grow up to embrace the truth about who she was to *unbecome* more than who she was to become. I believe that God divinely created scenarios in her life to shine a light on everything that He was to her and everything she was to Him. The more she learned about Him, the more she learned about her identity. The more things attached to her, the greater her need for His divine intervention grew. Had she not had all of the attachments, the attacks, the devil's personal interest, she would not need God's protection and unconditional love.

Never mind who the little girl was or who she became; I just want you to understand that our novice phase is vital. It is not because of the things we went through, but the things and ideas that attached to us. I'm a strong believer that God orchestrated our novice phase, and he blinded our eyes to certain things as well as opened our eyes to things that we needed to see in order for His divine will to come to pass.

It's imperative that we look back and take the things that we saw and the things that we experienced that actually attached to us, to evolve and elevate our minds to the next level. By looking at the beginning, we can get a glimpse of our backstory's original state, and we can identify traces of the wings inside the caterpillar. As long as we remember that we were given our wings when everything started, we will learn to appreciate our beginning and use it to keep flying as opposed to waiting for our wings to attach at a particular moment in time.

This is my declaration for our inception.
Looking back will only be a source of fueling our flight!

DETOX

"To absolve a thing from anything that is harmful to its evolution."

DETOX

Detox- to absolve a thing from anything that is harmful to its evolution.

One day, I was sitting at my desk, minding my business, when my coworker brought up the wonderful idea of starting a smoothie detox as a means of a team-building exercise. I was a bit heavier than I wanted to be, so I agreed. It was a 12-day smoothie detox. I was pumped because I was going to lose weight! Honestly, I didn't care about being healthier; I just wanted to lose weight.

Lesson: When thinking about our walk with Christ, there is a correlation between just wanting to lose weight versus actually being healthy. We are so full of zeal and hope when we first get saved. It is like we have won the jackpot. We are saved from sin, we have lost that weight, but are we spiritually healthy? Do we have the spiritual health we need to endure the walk?

Starting the detox was not an issue. The issue was being consistent. I started off great with my accountability partners. Then, my stomach touched my back for the first time, and it became a little harder to continue. My body had not been used to being deprived of certain fats, acids, and greases that I had been consuming for years. I literally had never detoxed before, and as my body was cleansing itself and being introduced to straight nutrients, it reacted differently to it.

The same thing happens when you start the *unbecoming* process. Things will physically feel different. You will want to go back to how you were doing things because a certain craving is being starved, and you're being cleansed from the inside out. You're ridding your mind of things that have attached themselves to your being. You are taking off the labels. Your mind is being transformed. Your stamina and discipline are building with every craving that you starve. It is not an easy process, but it is necessary to begin *unbecoming*.

I remember wanting a burger so bad in the middle of my detox, and I thought that I was able at least to cheat a little bit on my commitment to myself. There are times when we cheat ourselves out of commitments that we have made to ourselves. It would be different wiggling your way out of a commitment to someone else, but why do we cheat ourselves from growth? We say that we're going to fast and never do. We say that we're going to leave those toxic relationships alone, but we still send the "hey bighead" texts. We say that we're going to be more financially disciplined and not eat out as much, but we slide through a drive-thru because we've convinced ourselves that we've done good so far and we need a reward.

We fail at following through because we don't see the value in the process. We don't see value in the process because we've seen others go through processes carrying loads of things, and we don't know what true freedom is, nor do we know what to do to obtain it. Every time that we choose to cheat ourselves out of our growth/commitments, more pain will meet us during the process. Still, there is good news even though we cheat ourselves at times, once we make a conscious decision to *unbecome* and detox, our bodies know how to get us back into alignment. So, there is STILL purpose, even in the pain that we cause ourselves.

So, I bought a burger, and nothing was like the physical pain I felt in my stomach the next day after I had cheated myself. It felt like someone was stabbing me in the stomach with a steak knife. I could not sit still. I could not mask the pain that I was feeling. I wanted to fall on the floor and curl up in a ball.

My body reacted this way because it knew that those toxins had no place in my system anymore. Although my mind became weak and backtracked, my body got me back into alignment with my commitment. The same thing goes for your commitment to living a better life by *unbecoming* traditions you once followed and mindsets that you've taken ownership. Every part of you is involved in the process, so if your mind gets out of line, your body will realign itself and vice versa. In other words, although you feel like you've bitten off more than you can chew with a job or project, you still get up early to start your work. If your body gets out of line, your mind will correct itself. Meaning, although your body is physically tired, and you feel like it's shutting down, you focus your mind on finishing and pacing yourself.

When I had finished the entire detox, I felt so accomplished. I lost ten to fifteen pounds, and I thought that I was done. Little did I know that the purpose of the detox was to reset and keep the toxins out, not just do it to say I can detox. While you're on this journey, it's not to say that you've completed the checklist of things to do. It's to maintain the momentum and continuously find ways to live healthier.

Take this detox to another level. Find ways to become lighter. I have challenged myself to voice my feelings. I've made it a part of my detox because, for years, I had shut up. I stopped sharing my feelings and my perspectives on things and situations because I felt that they didn't matter. In a previous portion of my detox, I realized how toxic that perspective was.

My perspective is a gift, and although it wasn't always appreciated, I had no right to deprive myself of sharing my gift. So, I'm sharing. I will not be quiet at my expense. I will see the value of my thoughts and feelings, and I will not downplay said thoughts and emotions to please others' perceptions. That is MY challenge. Create a challenge for yourself and track your progress.

My Detox Challenge

Another one of the ways that I detoxed was I began to plan more. I wanted to make a conscious effort to accomplish whatever I wanted. This required a new level of discipline that stretched me, and it did not feel good. The fact of the matter remains that detox does not FEEL good. Therefore, we must understand that we aren't going to be FEELING every part of this process.

There were times when I didn't want to plan because I actually held myself accountable to carrying out whatever plan I set, and if I failed, it was just another thing that I was not good at. Also, there were times that I didn't want to plan because it would only add to the anxiety I was feeling about my life not being what I wanted it to be.

If you can identify with one or both of those reasons for not planning, CAUTION: SLOW DOWN! This is a process. It's not meant for you to plan to have everything figured out, but you must "ponder the path of your feet and let all your ways be established" (Proverbs 4:26 NKJV), understanding that "a man's heart plans his ways but the Lord direct his steps" (Proverbs 16:9 NKJV). So, plan. Have some direction about what you're doing, and watch how things begin to come apart and flow together.

Not only did I have to plan, but I also had to pray. Man, did I have to pray! The Bible says in Philippians 4: 6-7, "Be anxious for nothing, but in everything by prayer and supplication, with thanksgiving, let your requests be made known to God; and the peace of God, which surpasses all understanding, will guard your hearts and minds through Christ Jesus." NKJV There was literally no other way that I could get the peace that I needed. I could get prayers and prophecies, but it wasn't until I laid on my face seeking God's face that I felt the solace that I was seeking to keep going. Through prayer and meditation, I found that I had more baggage than ever. At times I thought that I was okay, then out of nowhere, depression would hit me like a ton of bricks.

Lesson: JUST because something comes up to tempt you does not mean that you aren't delivered from it. I remember being tempted with depression after publicly professing that I had never dealt with depression before. I was sober in my response because it was the truth. When I left the place where I professed this good thing, it was like the depression light switch flipped, and I was left standing in the middle of the room naked.

I experienced the "why" questions. Why me? Why get up? Why go to work? Why live? Why keep going? Where's God? Is God even real? Maybe I'm crazy. I'm all alone. Nobody cares. I'm tired. I'm tired of being tired. I'm tired of caring. I hate my job. I hate my life. I'm sick of this. These were very real thoughts in a very real-time in my life.

Although I experienced the realness of these thoughts, I didn't understand that the enemy will tempt you after you make a profession. I had been prepared for a time, such as that time. So, I did not stop praying. I kept getting up. I kept hoping. I did not stop. I encourage you to NOT stop and PRAY!

I needed deliverance from so many things from my past. Things I had suppressed for so long that I forgot some were even there. I forgot about the time that I felt forced to have sex when I really didn't want to, and my body reacted, so I thought, "I must have wanted it." I forgot about the time I was paid to keep quiet. I thought, "if I say something, my whole world will change, so I'll just keep it to myself." I packed away the times that I let a man devalue me because I thought I loved him. I thought, "love endures, right?"

I tucked away so many things and never had a release, but God. There was a time when I did not know what words to pray out loud. Unlike Hannah, I didn't even know what words to mouth. I just knew I needed all that He had to offer because I felt that I had nothing. Little did I know, I had everything. You don't have to say your best prayer. You don't need a lot of fancy words. Sometimes, you aren't even going to have the words, but pray, even if it is with a sound. He hears you, and He will answer you.

Another way that I detoxed was by saying, *NO, A LOT.* I've had to overcome people's expectations of me in so many different areas, including what I should do with my time and money. I'm the type of person that likes to support my loved ones in every endeavor, in any way I can. I gave so much emotionally, monetarily, spiritually to my loved ones and was left to depend on God and people who I didn't know very well to help me when I was in need. Of course, it's not all bad being the dependable person, but it gets lonely and leaves you unsettled when the tables turn, and you are in need, and the people you helped are not able to help.

So, I said *No.* If I didn't want to do something, I said *No.* I didn't make commitments that were outside of my area of contentment. When I couldn't say No, I didn't respond. Now, that may not have been the best thing to do, but I did it. I valued my "*No*" because it signified me taking back control of myself. I was no longer going to navigate life intoxicated.

Whenever you do something that you know you shouldn't do, or you succumb to actions that aren't "you," then you're intoxicating yourself. What does an intoxicated person do? They have blurred vision. Their balance is off. Their speech is impaired. They're overall dysfunctional. Imagine moving through life intoxicated from the resentment you picked up when the people you cared about walked away; the anger and sadness that settled inside of your soul when you lost a loved one; the shame that beset you when your plan failed. You became intoxicated. You needed a hard reset, a detoxification.

The most vital part of my detox was the "throwing up" stage. Sounds gross, right? Well, gross as it sounds, it's my truth. There were things that I couldn't drink away. I couldn't eat healthy enough for them to disappear. I couldn't take a detox pill to get rid of them. I legitimately had to throw them up. Of course, this throwing up had nothing to do with food, but I had to decide to share my past with people.

I had to relive moments so that I could "throw up" everything that I felt in those moments. The feeling of not wanting to rock the boat. The fear of people's perceptions, the fear of being neglected, the pressure to have it together, and to make the right decisions at all times. I had to confess my deepest secrets. The secrets that brought me shame. I had to throw them up. I didn't share all of my secrets with one person. I truly believe that God chose the people with whom I shared each moment. I would be lying if I said that shame was never present when I shared my moments, but because I was met with no judgment, I believe that a link to the chain broke every time I shared. Soon, shame left, and I was left with me; Just me. Empty me. Naked me. Shameless me. Healed me, and Recovering me.

It is amazingly freeing when you are alone and naked, yet strong. Paul said, Each time he said, "My grace is all you need. My power works best in weakness." So now I am glad to boast about my weaknesses, so that the power of Christ can work through me. That's why I take pleasure in my weaknesses, and in the insults, hardships, persecutions, and troubles that I suffer for Christ. For when I am weak, then I am strong." (2 Corinthians 12:9-10, NLT).

We are afraid to run on "E," but when we're on "E," God's power is on "F." We panic when it seems like everything is out of control. FYI: It is out of *YOUR* control. When you feel powerless, His power is at an all-time high. Empty yourself from every enslaving thought, feeling, idea, perception, and concept.

I hope that you detox and you break free from all of your past chains. Dig deeper. There is more. Ultimately, understand that God knew that you were going to get intoxicated. He knew that you would have blurred vision, and He is still saying that His grace is sufficient.

Dear Lord, we love you, God. You are amazing, and we worship you right where we are, for You are all we need. You know where we are, God. You know how we got here. Now God, show us the way. Show us who we can talk to; prepare them now to receive all that we have to dump out. Please give us the wisdom to speak when it's time to speak and tell us when to say less. You are our Ruler. You have this thing in control, and we trust You. We don't mind running on E so that we can experience your F. Have your way, God, in Jesus' name we pray, Amen.

"The most accurate representation of me lies within the pieces of glass plastered on the pages of the Bible."

MIRRORS

The most accurate representation of me lies within the pieces of glass plastered on the pages of the Bible.

It's the story of the Samaritan woman at the well when Jesus asked her where is her husband, and then he proceeded to read her like the book that contains this story (John 4-4:36). Sis was me. No, I had never been married, but I was looking for something. I believe that the woman was also looking for something, and she ended up getting more than she could have ever imagined. The best part of this story was that the Bible says that Jesus had to go through Samaria, and it doesn't tell of another encounter but the one involving the woman at the well, which means that God had her on His mind.

Mirrors can be so tricky at times. There are those that magnify all of your flaws, as well as those that light up just right so that your flaws are drowned. Some mirrors make you look a bit more round/thick (if you will) than average, and also, some make you look slimmer than normal. The general idea of a mirror is that it shows an accurate representation of what you look like at any given moment, but I just proved that not all mirrors function properly.

I cannot stress how important it is to have a functional mirror during this process. This means to find out what God says about you and how He's known for handling people like you. Read the Bible stories, find one or some that you can identify with, study it, and study the people involved. The Word says that there's nothing new under the Sun, which means to me, that I am not alone. There was someone who thought like me and acted like me; I just have to find them and put some language to the path I am trying to navigate. So seek the Word of God for examples, and you will find someone like you and learn how God dealt with them in order to learn how He desires to deal with you.

I've spent a great deal of my younger years studying other people and mirroring what I saw, and repeating things that I had heard. Obviously, it is natural because we have the saying "monkey see, monkey do." Well, I've decided that I'm not a monkey. I don't have to mirror someone else's behavior to be acceptable. There is not a perfect way to speak or act. Ultimately, we should try our best to mirror the image that has already been given to us by Jesus.

I found out that I was representing someone else's mirror when I was dating someone, and I found myself altering things that I liked to satisfy what I thought they wanted. Even if it made me uncomfortable or hurt me, I would go along with it because I was trying to portray an image of who I thought they wanted instead of being one hundred percent me. I would add filters to myself to match a mirror that was not mine.

My reflection was not good enough for me, so how could it be good enough for anyone else? I am not very ladylike, I do not always say what is right, and I don't always do what is right. I'm not particularly eager to cleaning all of the time. I like to cook, but I'm afraid to feed you because of the person I'm representing. Besides, if you don't like it, my representation's feelings would be hurt, and I'd silently tell you to cook it yourself next time, then offer to order takeout.

Listen, there have been so many battles that I've fought within myself to just "say it, Tiana," or "do it, Tiana," to be unapologetically me. My representation says that I should be apologetic if it's not what other people expect when truthfully, people are only expecting me to be me—nothing more, nothing less. I've done so many people an injustice by representing a compilation that I've made of the perfect woman instead of echoing the words to God, "Thank you for making me so wonderfully complex! Your workmanship is marvelous—how well I know it."(Psalm 139:14, NLT). I am the perfect woman because God made me. My ways may not be your ways or ways that you stamp with approval, but they're what makes me, me.

I remember resenting being physically attractive because that's all people would tie to me. I found myself defending who I was to everyone, young and old. I was thought of as "too good" or "conceited." So I believe I compiled parts from my perception of other women I admired, thinking that if I could mirror them just right, I wouldn't be judged as a conceited girl that doesn't need validation because she already has it. I resented the mirror. I resented my true representation, so I changed it. To be honest, it worked for a while. I thought that I was evolving, at least that's what I told myself. In actuality, I was just creating this other person and suppressing my true being. True bipolarism, if you ask me.

My true representation started to bubble over when I cursed out an ex so bad that the fake me and the real me were surprised. In my mind, he deserved it, but if I had not been trying to be this representation of the woman I thought he wanted, the real Tiana would've nipped the nonsense in the bud at the beginning of the relationship instead of simmering down and being the "good girlfriend." I needed to be a "real girlfriend." Boy, did he get it at the end, though!

Lesson: It shouldn't take a big blow-up for your real self to "bubble" out. You are enough, big mouth and all. You're exactly what people are looking for, friends, and companions alike. You don't have to change what you like to appeal to ANYONE. Who is for you will be for you, no matter what.

So, what do you do if you have identified yourself within

this chapter? Ask yourself, "Self, do you like you?" If you could change three things about yourself, what would they be?"

1._____
2._____
3._____

Now, the next question is key, and it is, "Why?" Why do you want to change those things? Is it because someone deemed that characteristic to be undesirable?

_____
_____
_____
_____

Don't let their preference alter your perception of yourself.

Now, take the three things that you chose to change and ask yourself, "how can I make these qualities work for my good?"

_____
_____
_____
_____
_____

God did it. He made our imperfections work for our good. We messed up, but He worked it. Through Jesus, we have been given the same power, so you can make it work. Now, I'm not saying that you should never change or evolve or be better; what I am suggesting is that we should evaluate our "whys" behind the change. A lot of times, they will reveal areas where we need God's healing and deliverance.

Be encouraged to be your true self. Don't be a walking representation of a compilation of other people. Find out what your Creator says and thinks about you. I promise that it is all good and TRUE things. For the Bible says, "What is the price of five sparrows—two copper coins? Yet God does not forget a single one of them. And the very hairs on your head are all numbered. So don't be afraid; you are more valuable to God than a whole flock of sparrows." (Luke 12:6-7, NLT). Whew, that is relieving to me. God doesn't forget the sparrows, and I'm MORE valuable than sparrows. He has numbered the actual hair on my head, so why should I change anything to fit anyone else's preference?

"Giants exist at the corner of Fear Avenue and Growth Street."

GIANTS

Doubt, fear, Rejection, depression, anxiety, frustration, and anger are all the different ingredients to create a *Giant*. It's not always easy to identify the components to your unhappiness, but identification is the most essential part of the healing process. How does a person heal from something they don't know they have? Do you want to be healed? Do you want to be free? Once you've answered yes to these questions, it's time to identify the heart of the issue. Where did this bondage come from? How long have you been this way? I know I'm hitting you with a lot of questions that you may not have the answer to just yet. Don't worry! I got your back. I'm not going to leave you hanging.

I'm old enough to understand that happiness is an emotion, and we control our emotions. Most people don't realize that emotions can get much bigger and deeper than just surface traits. If we feel a certain emotion for so long without changing it, it becomes a part of our character. Please make yourself aware of your feelings, whether it be good or bad, and don't let them linger. People would like us to think that certain emotions are natural; well, I don't trust anything that combats what God says that I am. Natural is great until it comes against the Word of God. So, take inventory of your feelings. Embrace the good and combat the bad. What are you feeling right now? You might say hungry, tired, or maybe you're just okay. Now, ask yourself, "what am I going to do with this information?" Are you going to stay hungry although you have food in the house and you're capable of changing that feeling? Would you allow yourself to keep feeling tired although you have time to rest? Is being okay all that you want to be? If you've answered yes to any of those questions, contact me personally because I need an explanation.

It's not enough to just know the solution to the problem.

Take your knowledge and make it work for you. Cry but not as much as you want. Be angry, but not as much as you feel. I'm not saying muffle your feelings; I'm saying you have the God-given power and authority to control these things. Don't become so entangled in emotion without taking inventory of the backstory of the emotion. Untie the knots {knots being the reasons, explanations, or hindrances} to these emotions one by one. One of my old supervisors would say, "What's the knot?" Meaning what's keeping you from doing a certain thing.

Untying the knots is not easy, and naturally, you're going to tell yourself that it's okay to feel this way, and you should embrace it because this is the idea that we millennials are being fed. We're not entitled to depression just because it's natural. We're not entitled to anxiety just because it feels like we can't control it. Yes, these are very real things that come along with genuine feelings, but you have the power to get out of those places.

Now I know that many people are going to have mixed feelings about what I'm saying because it's not scientifically correct, nor is it meant to be. This is a challenge for you to defy the norm of accepting something that's not yours. What you have been graced with are keys to a literal endless well of possibilities. I'm sure you've forgotten, which is why you think it's okay to wallow in hopelessness and depression and just let it run its course. I've come to challenge some of you to take authority over these so-called natural feelings and remind others that the access is still granted. Use your keys.

Being in a bound or depressed place doesn't mean that you've done something wrong or you deserve to be in that lowly place. I believe that a lot of time people have to make sense out of things, so they'd rather tell you that you wouldn't be experiencing those feelings of lack and purposelessness if you would've made different decisions. No matter how you arrived at the place you're at, you're there and need coaching while you're there.

It's not that you've done anything terribly wrong and unforgivable that God just turned His back on You. It's not that you made a bad decision, and you're suffering the consequences. It's just that life has done what life does, and now it's time for God to do what God does.

I know that it feels as if you're in a dark tunnel or perhaps a hole so deep that you can't climb out. I need you to know that it's okay to ask for help. Yes, everyone does life and does it differently; however, God has placed people in your path who can do their life and help you do yours as well. I know that you don't want to put people in your business, but don't be deep about it. These people have been pre-selected by God to assist you during this time. No matter how you met them or how they will exit your life, you're going to have to slow down and absorb whatever you can from them. You're in this depressed state for a reason. Perhaps it's to get you to experience the comma and a period for a change. You've been a run-on sentence for some time now, and it has worked out for you, but now it is God's turn to do the work within you.

Next, be patient. I know. You hear this, you see this, you feel this very thing every day, but it's only for your good. I remember having a conversation with my mother about some frustration that I had been experiencing for some time. She calmly listened to my woes and all the grief that I was trying to communicate, and she responded with, "you need patience, Tiana." WHAT? Patience? I was patient. I waited. I had been waiting, and nothing was changing. Be patient with yourself. You are delicate. As much as you would like to think that you're so strong and can handle any and everything that comes your way, remember that you are not God. He has given us much power and authority, but only through Him. If you have been divinely placed in an uncomfortable situation, He will get the glory out of it if only you learn to be patient. Don't focus so much on the waiting, but the strokes you take every day to move forward. That means that you may not be working at the place you see in your future, but notice the progress you've made, whether internal or external. Even if it's just showing up to work on time. That is a stroke. The book may not be finished, but you typed a sentence last night. That is a stroke. Be patient with you. Don't let anyone, even if it is someone you trust with your whole life, rush you. They are not your God. You submit yourself to God and watch Him work things out in HIS perfect timing.

Show up. There are going to be days that you feel so detached from the real world that every bone in your body will want to be still, but don't let it. Just because you're patient with yourself doesn't mean you're supposed to literally just sit and wait. This is the time when you seek balance because something is imbalanced, which is why you're so far to the left of the mood radar. Try something different. Balance, for me, is accepting compliments when I feel like I don't deserve them. I'm sure that sounds ridiculous to some people. However, it's a real thing. When people gave me compliments, I'd do one of two things: combat it with my own negative perception or neglect to say thank you and compliment the other person. It's going out to a work outing even if I'm not feeling social. It's moving out of the way of myself. It's being productive when I want to be lazy. Balance, to me, is making sure that I'm not getting stuck in my ways. It is being versatile and open to new ways of thinking. (I'm working on it.)

Giants are people, places, or things that seem too big for you to handle. Right now, there's a giant in my life that I'm going to name *Yield*. I didn't know *Yield* existed for a while until I got waist-deep into this *unbecoming* thing. I had identified my knots and untied them. I was dealing with the broken pieces that I had found within my character and put them back together again. I was helping people understand where they are and pouring out what God had graced me to know. However, I was still arriving at an undesirable location. I was finally doing something that I felt was leading me in the right direction to my destiny, but I still felt empty and alone. It wasn't until I looked into the mirror and realized that I was flat out doing too much. I didn't leave any room for *Yield* to be a part of my life. Instead of yielding to God's plan, I took the piece of what God had shown me and walked it out from what I wanted the vision to mean. I left no room for God to give the increase.

I don't want you to think that it is incorrect to take what God has shown you and walk it out, but allow God to be God. He's the only one who can sustain the piece of the vision He's given you. The test was not to see if you'd walk it out but to see if you'd trust Him enough to give Him free rein over His idea. There are times when He doesn't provide A-Z, and then there are times when He's specific. I'm not telling you that we should do nothing; I'm telling you to always be on the lookout for Him, His signs, and His wonders. He's in everything that we see and experience, and your idea or way of accomplishing the task may not be His way. Contrary to popular belief, I believe that God takes some of us down a more complicated path because there are things that need to be worked out before we reach our destination. I've dealt with guilt, shame, anxiety, depression, rage, insignificance, rejection, violation, and the list goes on. I would love to tell you that I deserved everything that I went through, but I didn't, and those moments are why yielding is so important. The gray areas that no man could fathom are why we need to be open to God be God in our lives. Yielding, per Tiana's dictionary, is consciously releasing your control to God and allowing yourself to be vulnerable to Him. When your control is released, and you're vulnerable, God has free reign to twist and turn your life in whatever direction. To answer your question, no, the twists and turns will not always be fun; however, if you're having a hard time facing the giant of y*ielding*, know that it's just a sign that you are being restored. It hurts to have things burned out of and off of you. The Bible says, " I beseech you therefore, brethren, by the mercies of God, that ye present your bodies a living sacrifice, holy, acceptable unto God, which is your reasonable service." (Romans 12:1, KJV).

Giants Change

For a large portion of my life, *Inadequacy* was the biggest giant that I had ever faced. Everywhere I went, it followed. It showed up in work meetings when I'd know the solution to the problem, but the spirit of *Inadequacy* said that someone knew better than I did. It showed up in my relationships when I'd try to do my best to fit whatever my partner wanted, even if it compromised things and ideals I knew to be right. I wanted to be enough for everyone, even when everyone wasn't enough for me.

I've had a few deep, meaningful relationships in my life, and *Inadequacy* was always the guest of honor. I remember sitting across from an ex at a really nice restaurant having our Valentine's Day dinner. I had planned our entire day, which started at around ten o'clock in the morning. We were to get massages first thing, then have a quick lunch, because I had to get the room ready. After I got the room ready, we'd meet at the house where our overnight bags were packed, then I'd take him to the room for the grand surprise, a rose petal covered room with candles, then we'd get dressed up and have dinner. BOOM! Perfect plan.

Well, we woke up, argued, rode to the parlor in silence, got massages in silence, went home to get our bags; I left him to prepare the room, which was half done because of a time constraint, picked him up, went to the room, got dressed, argued, then went to dinner. Whew, I'm exhausted from just typing that. Nevertheless, I stayed positive, "Well, we have the rest of the night," I thought. There was an undeniable tension at dinner, but listen, I was FINE, and I remember thinking, does he not see everything that I have done for him? I had lost some weight, I did my hair, planned this "perfect" night just for him to look across the dinner table at me and say, "I don't think I'll ever be good enough for you." DUDE!! This is not the time! However, it was time. It was time for me to see *Inadequacy* in rare form. I just sat in silence, feeling like I had been punched in the chest. All of the thought, all of the effort, all of the time, all of the feelings I had put into, not only that night, but that relationship, only for him to show me how I felt about me. He told me that he thought he would never be good enough for me. The truth was that I didn't think that I'd ever be good enough for him or me.

Throughout that relationship and others, I'd always feel as if I'd never be enough. Of course, I had met *Inadequacy* long before this experience, but this experience is one that was pivotal in my *unbecoming* process. I didn't think that I would ever amount to the woman I wanted to be to him. So, I did what I thought he wanted, what I thought would make me more appealing to him as a mate and what I thought would make him see only me. I had gone through life and relationship after relationship trying to live up to an idea that was not me because I, alone, could never and would never be enough; at least, that's what I thought. My exes may have loved someone, but it wasn't me.

I left that relationship broken and once again feeling like I was not enough, and I would never be enough. I saw

Inadequacy for who she was, but I didn't know how to fix it. All I knew was that I wanted to be me again. So, the next encounter I had with the opposite sex, I was me. Truly, me. Of course, I was guarded, but I revealed what I wanted to without thinking that something may be deemed unattractive. I spoke up. I peeped game and called him on it. I didn't live in a box of anyone's expectations or perceptions. I was free. Most importantly, I was truthful.

Lesson: *Inadequacy* will trick us into thinking that we are doing ourselves and other people a favor by flying below the radar, not rattling cages, conforming to people's expectations, well expectations we think they have. When honestly, we're fooling ourselves and adding another brick to the wall in front of the mirror that shows us our true selves.

Honey, apologize to yourself. Right now! Say it with me, *your name* I'm sorry for thinking that you are not enough. I will actively pursue myself, and I will not allow my like for someone to compromise my pursuit. I am whole. I am fine fine, okay. There are things that I like and do that may not appease your tastebuds, but it's me. I won't continue adding things to sustain an idea that I've created from my dealing with *Inadequacy*. I am enough. I was enough. I will be enough. If my enough doesn't match with yours, I will no longer shave corners or carve curves in areas to fit your puzzle.

Defeating the giant of I*nadequacy* took a lot out of me, literally. It brought out the voice I thought I lost. I spent years stifling my true feelings about things to keep the disturbance at a minimum, but I ended up losing the value of my own thoughts. I'm sure this giant will present itself again, but I've defeated it once, which gives me the courage to know that I can do it again.

So, once you've identified the giant and its origin, it's time to look in the mirror. Don't do anything while you're looking. Just stand and look. This, too, is an essential part of the healing that is taking place. You have to be able to look at yourself in the state that you're in now. Notice the different curves and wrinkles in your face. Notice the look in your eyes when you're staring at yourself. Notice your posture. To most people, this may seem a little weird because it is. Being in this kind of bondage is weird too. So, match your situation's weirdness. Do something strange for a little piece of CHANGE! (Of course, I'm not talking about doing anything explicit for monetary exchange).

The purpose of you looking in the mirror is to take inventory of everything that is about to leave you. It's not enough to start this process and not know where you came from. You will not look the same once you're fully healed. **HOW BAD DO YOU WANT IT?**

PASSION

"Passion lies at the crossroads of desire and suffering."

PASSIONS

Passion lies at the crossroads of desire and suffering.

"I feel incomplete. I feel like I'm stuck. Is God really taking me places? I feel like I never complete anything. I know that I have the capability to get things done because I complete things for people all of the time. Am I being partial against myself? Why am I so comfortable with reaching other people's goals?"

Now, maybe it's just me who has asked themselves at least one of these questions. I highly doubt it, though. You're waking up every day showing up to a job that requires so much of you, and you never fail to meet and sometimes exceed the minimum standard. However, when taking a look at your personal life, you realize that you're falling short of the minimum standard you've set for yourself. Perhaps, we have not set a standard, which is why we're feeling unaccomplished.

The chapter is called *Passions* because a part of *unbecoming* is identifying our passions. What is it that fulfills us? If you could do anything in the world without the world's judgment, what would it be? Mine would be getting to know people. I'm interested in how people operate. I like being able to connect the dots between people's experiences and their traits. I also like helping people identify the connections and helping them live through them. I thoroughly enjoy candid conversations about life experiences and issues and such. I suppose you can say that I may be a bit socially awkward because I take long pauses in deep conversations. I don't speak just to say I said something because I'm calculating the possible effects of my responses on myself and the other person(s). However, you would never be able to tell because I've mastered masking my inquisitive face, and I've suppressed my thoughts that lead me into the black hole of endless questions, scenarios, and outcomes.

Masking ourselves is a common thing that we do because we're afraid of how people will perceive our non-poker faces. Personally, I've thought to myself how weird and "out there" my thoughts and ideas were. Just think about how much we'd accomplish and how fulfilled we'd be if we would drive full speed ahead towards our passions. For me, that means not suppressing the questions I have because I realize that my ability to question things is a gift. We've been taught to just do whatever you're told with no questions. I challenge every reader to think back to all of the things they have been told that went against their God-given passions. I question, I process, and I have a way with words. This is what makes me Tiana, and I've decided to work with my passions to fulfill them rather than against them and diminish slowly. That means that when I have a question, I ask. It means that I will continue thinking out plans instead of just jumping. I won't suppress my input on subjects that I've been graced to experience.

Our passions are pre-existing conditions that never go away. They are terminal. They don't have to be recognized by anyone but us to establish their validity. Once we are birthed into this realm in a perfect world, we are given a manual that spells out exactly what we are supposed to do and when we're supposed to do it. However, I have yet to read a manual entitled Tiana's Instructions that tell me to write a book, but it's happening. Writing is a passion. Articulating thoughts is a passion. It disrupts my psyche when I am not writing or can't put my thoughts into words. When I can't help someone get better, my mood is thrown off. Why? Because it's my passion to help.

We can't afford to let our passions lie dormant. It causes

chaos in our minds because we know that we should be doing more. We feel drained. Our minds are working overtime to fix the error in our behavior. It's like we're in the game Temple Run where there's literally no way out. We run and jump and slide only to get tripped up by something small. Why is it so hard to flow with our passions?

I remember I coordinated an event in 2013 called Belles Connect. Basically, it was meant to be an event to bring together young women from different backgrounds for an empowerment session. This was a vision that God gave me, and by His grace, I was able to gracefully walk it out. He connected me with people to help me bring His vision to life, and it was all that it was meant to be. It was during the anonymous Q and A that I realized how internally weak I was. How ironic is it that I would be in the process of doing what God had called me to do and feel weaker than I have ever felt? I found the answer to be listed in my favorite book 2 Corinthians 12:9-10, "But he said to me, "My grace is sufficient for you, for my power is made perfect in weakness." Therefore I will boast all the more gladly about my weaknesses, so that Christ's power may rest on me. That is why, for Christ's sake, I delight in weaknesses, in insults, in hardships, in persecutions, in difficulties. For when I am weak, then I am strong."(NIV) My friends, this is great news for those of us with pre-existing passions. He gave us these passions for Him to manage. It's a challenge to believe that we have been given something that is not our full responsibility because you think that you're in control. Therefore, it's so hard for us to flow with our passions. Once we understand that we are just characters in a narrative much bigger than us, then we will be free from the weight called "Control."

I honestly believe that a large percentage of people in Christ carry control. Carrying control is believing that you have the power (maybe God-given) to control the outcomes of situations in life. Here's the thing, we all have choices to make. In order to make those choices, we have to weigh our options, meaning seek God. The truth is, our version of seeking God is asking our parents or close friends their opinions of our options. Did you know that God is so all-knowing and powerful that even if you made the wrong choice, (1) He knew which choice you'd make, and (2) He's already made it work for your good? Now, this isn't to say that you shouldn't seek God because He already knows what you're going to do. The Word says, "But seek first his kingdom and his righteousness, and all these things will be given to you as well." (Matthew 6:33, NIV) This is to declare that if you seek God in every transaction of your life, it will activate your faith to believe that God will make your choice produce great things because you sought Him. Carrying control doesn't require faith. It just requires us to think with our small minds about possible outcomes that we don't fully understand because there's a greater story at stake. Our eyes are not high enough to make sure that we're in line with how the story is supposed to go.

Another passion that I have is communicating. I've attended webinars and took detailed notes just so I could get better at my passion. I remember feeling so inadequate because I didn't have anything that I liked to do with my hands. I mean, I could do hair, but I didn't LIKE to do hair. I could sing, but not good enough for a record deal. I could dance, but I'm not real athletic. There were things that I could do, but it was never something that I thoroughly enjoyed doing. I was in a class once, and the question was asked, "Well, what are you good at?" My response was "talking," and we all laughed, but it was the truth. I was good at communicating. Of course, back then, I didn't know that a person could have a gift of communication, so I left that conversation questioning my skillset. However, now I realize how communication affects so many parts of our lives, and I take pride in the passion that God has given me to communicate well with others.

Having the language to communicate my thoughts and feelings, and processes is very important to me. So, I'm always looking for new words, new languages to add to my library to communicate better. I listen to how people express themselves and evaluate their choice of words and what I believe their underlying message to be. Honestly, it's not as weird as it sounds. I've learned that since I've come to understand my passions, some people don't want to learn the language that you speak, and that's okay. Keep speaking your language fluently because someone with an ear and heart is open to learning your language because they need some of your words to fix their broken language.

For me, this lesson was a testament to how passions will not always be understood, even by the people in your innermost circle. I remember sharing some of my passions with someone very close to me, and I was met with a dry, "oh, that's good." "WHAT?!" I exclaimed on the inside. I was looking for more, criticism, enthusiasm, any other -ism, but all I received was a "that's good" I felt deflated. I'm already closed off, and now, I'm actually trying to be more open, and I'm met with everything less than what I expected.

That initial feeling left after I shared my aspirations a couple more times with different subjects. Some responded with a plan of action. Some responded with encouragement. Others just stuck with the "that's good." Some people would say, "that is why you have to be careful of who you share your vision with," while that may be true, a different lesson was waiting to be learned by me. I learned that responses shouldn't guide my level of commitment and dedication to my passion. I won't stop sharing because someone's response is less than my expectation. Truthfully, if their response does not contribute in some sort to the development of my passion, it reveals that they do not speak my language on that topic, which is fine. Keep speaking, though. Don't shut down. A certain group of people needs you to share so that their passions can be activated or developed.

The only other instruction that I want to suggest to you is: Don't leave out ANYTHING. You are not incomplete. You have all of the pieces. For the Bible says, "After everyone was full, Jesus told his disciples, "Now gather the leftovers, so that nothing is wasted." (John 6:12, NLT). There are leftovers. So, whatever you thought was not of use, whatever you thought was picked over by others, whatever you thought you could not use, as it pertains to your passions, please do not leave it out. Gather all of the experiences you have, all of the gifts you've been given, and ultimately everything you LOVE to do and do it; Period. There's no need to measure yourself up to anyone else and their progress working out their passion because you have your work cut out for you within your own arena. Take all of your scraps, pick a piece, and start. Just as if we were dealing with giants, we're going to take a stroke.

What is your goal? Do you want to make money? Do you want to just help people? Next, how can you accomplish your goal? If your goal is to make money, research ways to monetize your gift. If your goal is to help people, research ways to build an audience and get your content seen/heard so that you can help. Who is your audience? Each question that you come up with and answer is a stroke. Every time you Google or search for YouTube tutorials or instructions, you're taking a stroke. I need you to understand that you're not stuck. Focus on what God has given you, and multiply it. There's not a "how" manual, which is great because you can do this your own way! There's no box that you HAVE to fit in because this is your process in passions.

TODAY

"IS THE MOST RECENT DEFINITION OF WHO AND WHAT I AM, BUT IT COULD NEVER DEFINE WHO I WILL BE."

TODAY

"Today is the most recent definition of who and what I am, but it could never define who I will be."

Sometimes we wait on the validation of men to take a step towards something we want. We wait for them to acknowledge the existence of our greatness because we are not ready to be great. People who are prepared to be great don't wait for someone to give them a chance to be great... it's embedded in their walk and talk and ways. They don't have to seek an approval or an "amen" because it's who they are. They can't contain it, they can't hide it, and they don't try to. I'm aiming to be the greatness that I feel without other people's involvement. Some people like to pose the choice of doing something with or without, but I'm saying without because if I say with, I just might wait and look back to see if you're with me, and that's unacceptable. So, I won't share my opinions or plans to get input, I will share for your knowledge because if I can see it, then I can do it, and I see it, so I'm going to do it.

Today, I cried. I stood in the shower and silently ugly cried. I know that God hears my prayers. He answers them daily. I've come so far from where I was, yet I still cried. It was an emotional response to the love of God that I experience daily, but for the first time in a long time, I allowed His love to capture me in my most intimate place. A place that no one can enter but Him because he created it. It is the secret place that I asked him to let me dwell in 10 years ago. I thought that it was a destination that he would grant me access to when it is actually a place that he created within me that I have to allow Him to enter.

My secret place held all the doubt, fear, *Rejection*, violation, judgments previously mentioned. It's all but a pretty place to dwell. Although God didn't give me these things, He created a place for them so that He can relieve me from them. I have to continually allow Him into that place to heal, deliver, and set me free. It is in that place from whence all the words written in this book flow.

It's ironic how the Lord revealed to me the book title *unbecoming* because I knew from past use of the word that it couldn't be positive. I imagined this book being a positive token describing life from my perspective. *Unbecoming* basically means ugly. After looking up the documented definition, my thoughts were: "what does that have to do with anything that I've written? I thought, "that can't be right." It's like when you're trying to turn up your spiritual ears, like God, are you sure? Did I hear you right? Then it dawned on me; this is not flattering. The secret place is dark and ugly. The process that I'm going through is very unattractive. It's quite painful internally, and the inevitable external factors weigh a bit more heavily than normal.

My reactions to the changes that I've been going through since the revelation of *unbecoming* have hurt some of my friends and family. It's not that I've been less loving, but I've been more me. I feel that it's important for us to understand that with great change comes great change. It sounds ridiculous and redundant, but what I mean is that once we decide that we are going to change, change will find us. For example, if I decide to like my job, I've made space in my mind for change to take place. I'm not just taking it as it comes and letting my emotions lead me into thinking that I don't like my job. Therefore, I'm going to work conscious of my decision to like my job and allowing God to give the increase of actually changing my mind. It's the decision to change that brings change.

Change manifests in different ways. For me, I'm less worried about what people think of my decisions. I don't take on other people's problems anymore. Although I'm an impeccable problem solver, I try to leave the God work to God. I don't do, just because I can. I live freely and comfortably within the area of grace and faith God has given me.

The great thing about this process of change is that it's yours. I can not tell you what your change will or will not be. However, you will recognize the change(s). Some things will be sudden, while others will be gradual and/or continuous. The good news is both are equally effective and necessary.

Change is not always easy, and you will not welcome every change with open arms. I remember getting into a heated argument with my stepfather. It was to the point where I questioned my whole family's loyalty. I felt that justice was not shining on my situation, and I cut everyone off. I spoke to my mom, but I felt different inside. I knew that change had slapped me in the face. I, now, had choices to make. Was I supposed to disconnect from the people that I knew and loved forever? Was I the problem? If there was to be reconciliation, how would that happen after so many unpleasant words were exchanged?

At this time, I was living in my parent's house. I paid my bills. I took care of my responsibilities. How could I be the issue this time? The short answer was that I NEEDED to be the issue this time. I had a chance to choose wholeness and honor versus bitterness and deceit. My time was up from living with my parents. I needed to trust that God was going to provide for me. The crutches had to be taken away violently for God's will to be done. My mom always said that He'd burn the nest if it's time for you to go.

This time, I prayed for God to heal my heart. I didn't want to hate anyone. I wanted to be able to forgive wholeheartedly. I wanted to be able to trust again. I needed restoration for my family. God delivered on every prayer that I cried out to him during this change. The change resulted in a sporadic move. The change resulted in my total independence from people and transitioned me to a dependence on God. I didn't want that change. I thought I was fine where I was, but God had more in store for me. He restored my relationship with my family. Forgiveness flourishes in my heart.

Our change processes are ours, and so many forms of change are flowing through us, we have to protect them. When God reveals a new level of wisdom and knowledge to us, we want to share it with everyone we know without considering if their souls can actually comprehend the messages we try to convey. Not that we literally have time to discern whether a person can handle us and our wild thoughts. However, I believe that an indicator of the imbalance would be the presence of loneliness when you have all of these wonderful thoughts, ideas, and concepts, but your environment's vantage point (caterpillar) is too low to understand the heights (butterfly) that your mind has reached.

There is a freedom that comes when you share with people who may not be able to relate directly, but they can process what you're saying and give credible feedback that actually feeds your initial idea, whether that be making you think more on the idea, or revealing a different perspective of the idea, whatever it may be just make sure that it is positive.

If God had told me that I would have to go through so many changes to get to this place, I probably would've dropped the cross, but Christ didn't, even though He knew what was to come. So I assume the position, as a wise man once shared with me. We should understand that we won't always know what is to come, but one certain thing is that there will be highs and there will be lows, just as an EKG monitor. Your heart rhythm shows up to a normal person as a zig-zag line that has high points and low points.

I've studied the parts of the EKG, and I've learned that the zig-zag line that non-doctors and non-nurses are referring to is made up of several different parts and pieces that signify very different things. There's the P wave, the QRS where R is listed as the peak, and then the t wave then you have different intervals and segments that are labeled. I thought this was very interesting because you have this reading that is virtually a line that tells the nurses and doctors information about our hearts and our life. In the movies, we've gotten accustomed to hearing the long beeping noise and seeing the flat line when someone dies. It's ironic how a medical machine is programmed to read your life with ups and downs, always returning to its original line only to rise again. Studying the EKG machine reading made me realize that everything isn't going to be a straight line. My process, my accomplishments, my personal growth are not defined by just one straight line. They are defined by ups and downs and waves that signify my existence. So, I embrace the waves and my QRS. If everything were just a straight line, I'd be dead, but instead, here I am, alive and well.

p.s.tianamarie

DIARY

"Nothing embodies a person's nakedness more than the words written in their diary."

DIARY

Nothing embodies a person's nakedness more than the words written in their diary.

Caution: Realness lies ahead in the excerpts from several of my diaries. Most of them are prayers, but some are just thoughts that I expressed on paper. Excerpt dates range from 2013 to 2020. I hope this act of transparency puts a real image in your head of the things I experienced. God delivered me every time I cried out. Not because I said the perfect words, but because He's God.

Disclaimer: These are not prayer templates.

___2013___

Keeping it all together when you feel like no one knows you, and even if they did know you, they wouldn't be able to fix the problem(s). Keeping it all together when stuff has been wrong so long that you thought wrong was right. Meeting new people but automatically shutting them out. They don't understand that you're just keeping it all together.

p.s. tianamarie

UNBECOMING

12/23/2013

Is it worth it? That's how I feel. Is what I'm doing going to pay me back? Am I just working myself for no reason? Life really does hit you fast, like a dang punch in the face sometimes. It hurts, it stings, it swells, it bruises, and it scars, but is the "extra" worth it? I'm so used to giving everything up because I'm quick to deem things and people unworthy of any more of me. I'm already scarred and bruised, so is it really worth it? Closing myself off from people refusing to open that door again. Afraid of what's behind the door or maybe what's NOT behind the door...

p.s.tianamarie

UNBECOMING

1/12/2014

We needed it! Every bit of it. Every tear that dropped, every beat that stopped, we needed it. Every person that left and ever promise unkept, we needed it. The thought of change never changed my pain, but I needed it. Covering, hovering, suffering from distress. All depressed from stuff I needed while I'm pleading for release. Oh, God help me, please! Thunder on the rumble everywhere that I stumble. There's no escape! I'm being raped from my authority and the courage to tell my story. I'm only wanting to give HIM glory! SILENCE. Exhaling, all the hell that's breaking loose. BREATHE. (All the anger, all the stress, all the hurt, all the shame) The mind games that were played are now in the few gray shades that I sway in between. Attitude, unexplainable 'cuz my freedom seems unattainable. My mind's bogged down, I'm up against a wall trying to stall the fall that I needed. I needed to see that it was bigger than me! So, I fell to my knees, praying my deliverer restores me. At His feet, I relinquished myself because the pain that I needed, needed to be released.

p.s. tianamarie

_____ 2016

I'm mad, God. There are no other words to describe my emotions this morning. I'm just mad. I'm trying to get my attitude in check, but it's taking longer than usual, so I figured if I tell you, then it will make it all better. I'm honestly tired of taking everything that people dish out to me and just swallowing it like I don't have feelings. Everything I go through tends to be much deeper than what it appears to be. Like I can cry on the outside but on the inside, I'm burning up. I don't miss this feeling, and I know that there are people who feel worse and are dealing with worse, but I'm just talking God. I know everything will be fine in due time, but I just wanted to be honest with You instead of spitting out regular prayers and thanks and blessings. You know the good, the bad, and the ugly already, so there's no reason to hide it. I'm a mess, and I want you to keep reminding me about how big of a mess I am so I won't ever get to a place where I think I'm "all good" I love You, Lord. In Jesus' name. Amen

p.s. tianamarie

_____2016_

There was a moment in time when all I want to be was invisible. I didn't want anyone to see me or my flaws, but I wanted them to see Your perfection. I was desperate really. I cried and cried because I'd become so messed up that I resorted to being invisible.

p.s.tianamarie

_____ 2016

I'm mad. I'm anxious and mad and overwhelmed, and I need Your presence. I thank You for all You've done and all You're doing and going to do. Things that didn't bother me bother me. People who didn't bother me bother me now. I want to feel joy and happiness, and I just don't feel that right now. I know it's not okay to feel this way, but I do. I want to quit. I want to give up everything. I feel like I've failed You and my kids. I want to be more patient and loving. I just feel I can do better in so many areas, and it's just not happening. I know that I'm in transition. I don't really know what that means, but it's happening. I just need to make it to the other side already. I'm just tired of trying everything right now. Is this what life is about? Is this it? Are my dreams too big? Am I trying to do too much?

_____ 2017

Why are you so afraid to take a risk that you're not responsible for? If you fail, it's not you failing; it's God's rerouting. Being rerouted is not always a bad thing. Inconvenient? Maybe. Frustrating? Maybe. All bad? Nah.

                                      p.s.tianamarie

5/14/18

Dear Lord, I don't always get it right that's why I need You. I need Your guidance and Your direction. I know You're with me. I know You're capable. Just tell me what to do. Speak clearly, God, so that I can't deny it's your voices I want to hear You like I've never heard You before. I want to move deeper in my relationship with You. You are the most important piece of my life Lord, and I need You! You're an amazing God, so merciful and gracious. Lord, I pray that whatever is stopping or may stop me from reaching my destiny... I pray that it be moved, Lord. No delays, God. I love you. In Jesus' name, I pray Amen

p.s. tianamarie

UNBECOMING

5/14/18

Dear Lord, I just want to take the time to tell You thank You for giving me visions and the motivation to work on these visions. I pray that the stakes are raised right now in the name of Jesus. I don't want to sit on or play with Your gifts I want to share them. I don't mind waiting, but I ask that you continue to prepare me and release me loud and clear when You're ready for me. You are the best Father ever, and I don't know what I'd do without You. I thank You for molding me now into a good thing a perfect thing for my earthly eternal love. I thank You now for restoring peace and joy and happiness to me. I thank you for mending my heart even now and allowing me to love only the person You created just for me with the deepest kind of love. Now Lord, prepare me. Remove all evil from around me. Anything that is not like You burn it up now I present my body as a living sacrifice God. Only to You! Mold me, break me, shape me, pick me up, and shake me up dust me off. I love You

God, and You are indeed amazing. I give You my everything. You are awesome. Please don't pass me by! In Jesus' name Amen.

p.s. tianamarie

UNBECOMING

_5/17/18_

Dear Lord, I thank You that I'm not the bitter person that I once was. Thank You that you delivered me from brokenness and healed me, and still healing me from the inside out. Thank You, God, for working patience within me at this very moment. I thank You because I can trust You. I trust you to do whatever You need to do in me to fulfill my destiny. I pray that you teach me how to fully surrender because I'm here and think I'm doing it, but I may not be so I need You to teach me how to do it right. I love You, God. You're an amazing God. You're so careful and loving, and I couldn't imagine life without you. You're the best, and I love You. Now, God, remove anything AND ANYONE who is not ordained by You for me. I really don't want it if it's not for me. I want whatever and whoever You have for me. Lord, I don't mind waiting. I know Your plan is perfect and worth it, so imma wait, and I'm not going to rush anything.

p.s. tianamarie

12/16/18

Psalm 104:14 for he knows how are formed, he remembers that we are dust. He knows your thought patterns. He knows why you have the thoughts you have; He knows why you have those thoughts about others and yourself. He knows what we are going through right now because it's a part of how we are being formed. He remembers what we came from; He remembers that we are dust and how we were created. Be confident in God's love for you. He knows everything. He's just great like that. Change your focus from you to Him because we've established that you aren't worthy. We've established that you're sinful. We've established that you have shortcomings, now shift your focus from being on you and your well-known unworthy self and focus on the almighty God, the one who knows your make up. Who was your Creator? Who knows how you will evolve and who holds your expected end in His hands? Oh, how great

You are God!

p.s. tianamarie

2/4/19

Lord, I'm sorry for being anxious. I'm sorry for letting things shift my focus. I'm sorry for not focusing my attention on you. I'm sorry for not always doing what's appropriate or saying what's appropriate and letting things that have no rights to me or my thought pattern to reside there. Thank you for never giving up on me. Thank you for cherishing me and for giving me value that no man can take away. Thank you for protecting me. Thank you for being there for me. Thank you for being consistent. Thank you for always being available. Thank you for fitting me into your schedule. Thank you for seeing me. Thank you for knowing me. Thank you for loving me and comforting me. Thank you for guiding me. Thank you for accompanying me on this journey. Thank you for enduring on my behalf. Thank you for allowing me to be me. Thank you for not condemning me. Thank you for being great. Thank you for being You.

You're everything that I need. You have everything that I need. I appreciate you, God, for it all. Thank you for teaching me. Thank you for calming me. Thank you for creating me. Thank you for all that you've blessed me with. Thank you, Lord. In Jesus name   Amen

p.s. tianamarie

<u>12/31/2020</u>

<u>Dear Lord, do Your thing. In Jesus' name,</u>
<u>Amen.</u>
<u>   p.s.tianamarie</u>

www.ingramcontent.com/pod-product-compliance
Lightning Source LLC
Chambersburg PA
CBHW070939160426
43193CB00011B/1746